MW00805614

This second book in the Master Thinking Skills series is designed to help young children continue to build thinking, and reasoning, skills. Exercises such as identifying same and different shapes, and activities requiring deductive reasoning provide an introduction to these critical skills. Other exercises include classifying, finding patterns and analogies, sequencing, alphabetizing and map-reading skills. Children also practice making inferences, predicting outcomes and other practical study skills.

Table of Contents

Glossary

Alphabetizing. Putting things in order.

Classifying. Putting things that are alike into categories.

Deductions. Using reasoning skills to draw conclusions.

Finding Analogies. Comparing similarities.

Finding Antonyms. Finding opposites.

Finding Homonyms. Finding words that sound the same but are spelled differently.

Finding Patterns. Recognizing similar shapes.

Inference. Using logic to figure out what is unspoken but evident.

Learning Dictionary Skills. Looking up words in the dictionary.

Predicting Outcome. Telling what is likely to happen based on available facts.

Same/Different. Being able to tell how things are the same and different.

Sequencing. Putting things in order.

Tracking. Following a path.

Same/Different

Directions: Look at the pictures. Put an **X** on the picture in each row that is different.

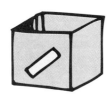   

3

Same/Different

Uncle Leo is fishing. He sees four sea monsters in the water. Three are the same. One is different.

Directions: Color the sea monster that is different.

Name: _____

Same/Different

Dapper Dog wants a new house. Help him find the shapes he needs.

Directions: Look at Dapper Dog's old house. Now look at the boxes of shapes. Which box has all the same shapes in it? Color those shapes.

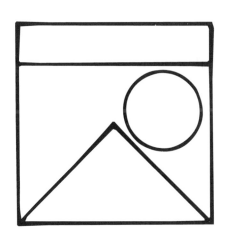

Name: _____

Making Deductions

Tom and Tess are looking for gold. They have found many shapes.
Which one has the gold in it?

Directions: Look at the shapes. Then answer the questions.

1. The gold is **not** in a yellow triangle △.
   Put an **X** on all the yellow triangles.

2. The gold is **not** in a circle ○.
   Put an **X** on all the circles.

3. The gold is **not** in a blue square □ .
   Put an **X** on all the blue squares.

4. The gold is **not** in a red star ☆.
   Put an **X** on all the red stars.

5. Circle the shape with the gold.

Name: _____

Making Deductions

Now Tom and Tess are late for dinner. What time is dinner?

Directions: Look at the clock. Then answer the questions.

1. It is now 6:00 p.m. Use an orange crayon for the clock's hands.

2. It was 3:00 when they left home. Draw the clock hands in blue.

3. Mother said, "Dinner is in two hours. Be home then." Draw the clock hands in purple.

4. What time were they to be home? _____

Name: _____

Making Deductions

Dad is cooking dinner tonight.

Directions: Look at the clues below. Fill in the menu. What day is it?

Menu	
Monday	_____
Tuesday	_____
Wednesday	_____
Thursday	_____
Friday	_____
Saturday	_____
Sunday	_____

1. Mom fixed pizza on Monday.

2. Dad fixed cheese rolls the day before that.

3. Tess made meat pie three days after Mom fixed pizza.

4. Tom fixed corn-on-the-cob the day before Tess made meat pie.

5. Mom fixed hotdogs the day after Tess made meat pie.

6. Tess cooked fish the day before Dad fixed cheese rolls.

7. Dad is making chicken today. What day is it? _____

Making Deductions

Directions: Use the clues to help the children find their books. Draw a line from each child's name to the right book.

CHILDREN	BOOKS
Tom	jokes
Tess	cakes
John	monsters
Jim	games
Lola	flags
Bill	space

Clues

1. John likes jokes.
2. Lola likes to bake.
3. Bill likes far away places.
4. Tess does not like monsters or flags.
5. Jim does not like space or monsters.
6. Tom does not like games, jokes or cakes.

Name: _____

Review

Directions: Look at each question. Follow the instructions.

1. Circle the box of shapes that matches Dapper's.

 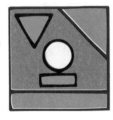 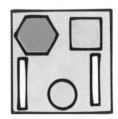  

2. Color the star that is exactly the same as the first star.

3. Who is eating lunch at the park? Answer the clues to find out.

1. Sue is on the swing. Put an **X** on Sue.
2. Mary is playing with Sue.
   Put an **X** on Mary.
3. Peter is not swinging.
4. Paul is sitting beside the boy
   eating lunch. Paul is not eating.
   Put an **X** on Paul.
5. Erin is on the sliding board.
   Put an **X** on Erin.
6. Who is eating lunch? _____

Name: _____

Classifying

Directions: Look at each leaf and read each leaf's name. Then follow the instructions.

white oak   silver maple   poison ivy   ash

Now write the name of each leaf under its picture. Color each leaf.

_____   _____

_____   _____

Name: _____

Classifying

Directions: Look closely at the tricky tree. It has four different kinds of leaves: ash, poison ivy, silver maple and white oak. Then follow the instructions.

1. Underline the white oak leaves .   How many are there? _____

2. Circle the ash leaves 🍃 .   How many are there? _____

3. Put an **X** on the poison ivy leaves 🍂. How many are there? _____

4. Box the silver maple leaves   How many are there? _____

12

Name: _____

Classifying

Poison ivy is not safe. If you touch it, it can make your skin red and itchy. It can hurt. It grows on the ground. It has three leaves. It can be green or red.

Directions: Watch out Dapper Dog! There is poison ivy in these woods. Color the poison ivy leaves red. Then color the other "safe" leaves other colors.

Name: _____

Classifying

Directions: Go outside and find some leaves. Put your leaves into groups. Do you know their names?

white oak

red oak

pine

ash

elm

silver maple

red maple

poison ivy

1. How many white oak leaves did you find?   _____
2. How many red oak leaves did you find?   _____
3. How many pine needles did you find?   _____
4. How many ash leaves did you find?   _____
5. How many elm leaves did you find?   _____
6. How many silver maple leaves did you find?   _____
7. How many red maple leaves did you find?   _____
8. Did you find any others?   _____
   Can you name them?

_____

_____

_____

Name: _____

Classifying

Directions: Circle the things on the menu that Dapper Dog will eat. He likes fruit and things made from fruit. He likes bread.

MENU	
apple pie	corn
peas	rolls
beans	banana bread
oranges	grape drink
chicken	

Name: _____

Classifying

Directions: Use a red crayon to circle the names of 3 animals you would want for a pet. Use a blue crayon to circle the names of 3 wild animals. Use an orange crayon to circle the 2 animals that are pests.

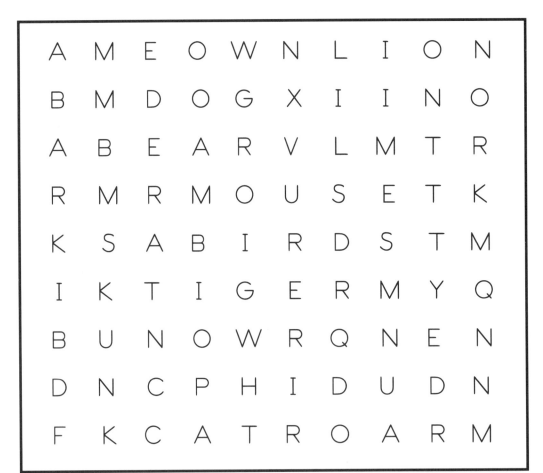

```
A  M  E  O  W  N  L  I  O  N
B  M  D  O  G  X  I  I  N  O
A  B  E  A  R  V  L  M  T  R
R  M  R  M  O  U  S  E  T  K
K  S  A  B  I  R  D  S  T  M
I  K  T  I  G  E  R  M  Y  Q
B  U  N  O  W  R  Q  N  E  N
D  N  C  P  H  I  D  U  D  N
F  K  C  A  T  R  O  A  R  M
```

Classifying

Dapper Dog is going on a camping trip.

Directions: Put an **X** on the word in each row across that does not belong in that group.

1.	flashlight	candle	radio	fire
2.	shirt	pants	coat	bat
3.	cow	car	bus	train
4.	beans	hotdogs	ball	bread
5.	gloves	hat	book	boots
6.	fork	butter	cup	plate
7.	book	ball	bat	milk
8.	dogs	bees	flies	ants

Name: _____

Review

Directions: Follow the instructions for each question.

1. Look at the leaf on the left. Now look at the pictures of the other 3 leaves. Write the missing name under the leaf.

_____   red oak   poison ivy   ash

_____   silver maple   elm   white oak

2. Color the pictures that are fruit.

apple   beans   corn   peach

3. Put an **X** on the word in each group that does not belong.

night   black   dark   sun

ash   oak   rose   elm

bread   banana   rolls   muffin

Name: _____

Finding Patterns

Directions: Finish each row with the right shape.

     _____

      _____

      _____

  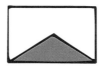 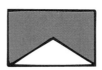 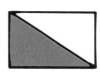 _____

Name: _____

Finding Patterns

Directions: Look at each shape. Use a crayon to trace the shape of any letter you see inside it.

M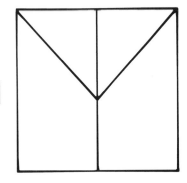

T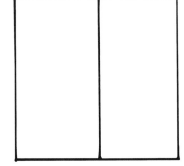

D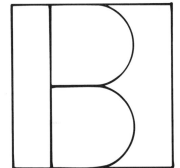

O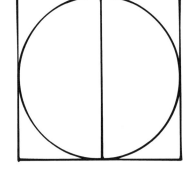

B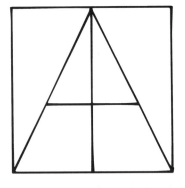

P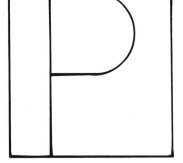

A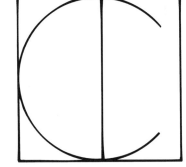

C

Name: _____

Finding Patterns

Directions: Look at the box on the left. Find the box on the right that has the same pattern of shades in it. Draw a line between the two.

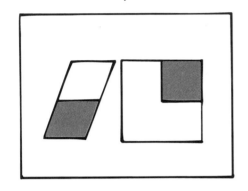

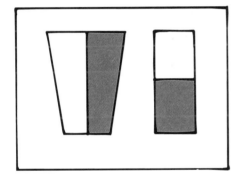

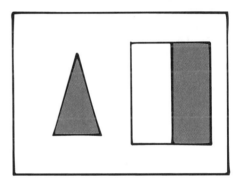

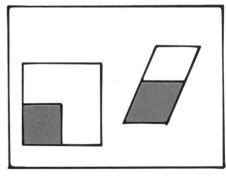

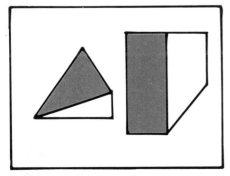

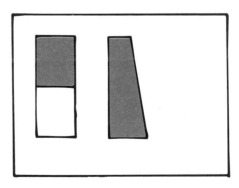

Name: _____

Finding Analogies

Example:

A little triangle is to
a big triangle

as

A little circle is to
a big circle

Directions: Look at each set of shapes. Draw the shape to finish the analogy.

as

  _____

as

  _____

as

  _____

Finding Analogies

Directions: Look at the shapes. Draw the shape that finishes the analogy.

  as _____

 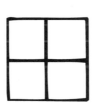 **as** _____

  as _____

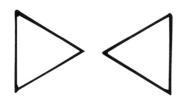 **as**  _____

23

Name: _____

Finding Analogies

Directions: Look at the shapes on the left. Find the shapes that finish the analogy on the right. Draw a line between them.

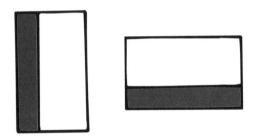

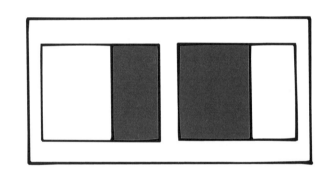

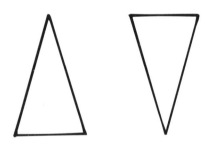

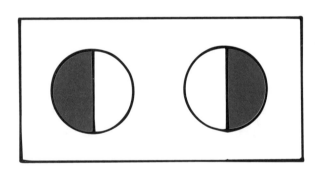

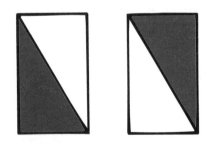

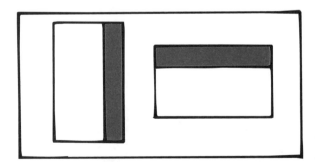

Name: _____

Finding Analogies

Directions: Look at the shapes on the left. Draw two shapes to complete the analogy.

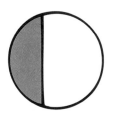 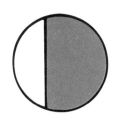 as _____

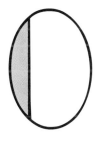 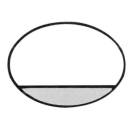 as _____

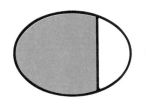  as _____

  as _____

25

Name: _____

Review

Directions: Look at each question. Follow the instructions.

1. Trace **M** as many times as you can find it.

 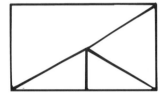  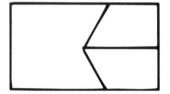

2. Complete the pattern in the last square.

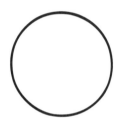 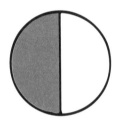  _____

3. Look at the first three shapes. Draw a shape that completes the analogy.

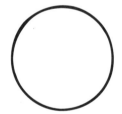  as  _____

4. Make an analogy to the shapes below.

  as _____

Name: _____

Sequencing

Tom and Tess are making a snack. They are fixing nacho chips and cheese.

Directions: Look at the picture. Then look at the steps that Tom and Tess use. They are all mixed up. Help Tom and Tess decide what to do first. Put the numbers beside each sentence to tell them which steps come first. Then color the picture.

_____ Tom and Tess cook the chips in the oven for 2 minutes.

_____ They get out a plate to cook on.

_____ Tom and Tess get out the nacho chips and cheese.

_____ Tom and Tess eat the food.

_____ They put the chips on a plate.

_____ They put cheese on the chips.

Name: _____

Sequencing

Directions: Kate is sick. What do you think happened? Put numbers beside each sentence to tell the story.

_____ She went to the doctor's office.

_____ Kate felt much better.

_____ Kate felt very hot and tired.

_____ Kate's mother went to the drug store.

_____ The doctor wrote down something.

_____ The doctor looked in Kate's ears.

_____ Kate took a pill.

_____ The doctor gave Kate's mother the piece of paper.

_____ Kate drank some water with her pill.

Name: _____

Sequencing

Directions: Dapper Dog wants to make a new friend today. Help him by putting in order the steps for meeting the little boy in the picture.

_____ Dapper Dog kisses his mother good-bye.

_____ Dapper Dog sees the new boy next door.

_____ Dapper Dog goes outside.

_____ Dapper Dog says hello.

_____ Dapper Dog gets dressed and eats breakfast.

_____ Dapper Dog wakes up.

Sequencing

Mrs. Posey is making a new hat.

Directions: Mrs. Posey has her story all mixed up. Read her story. Now on the lines below it write the story in the order that you think it happened. Color the picture.

Mrs. Posey's story:

I stuck flowers onto it.
Then I bought this straw hat.
Now I am wearing my hat.
I tried on many hats at the store.

Your story:

_____
_____
_____
_____
_____
_____
_____
_____
_____
_____

Name: _____

Alphabetizing

Sometimes words are put into ABC order. That means that if a word starts with A, it comes first. If it starts with B, it comes next, etc.

Directions: Look at each row of pictures. Circle the picture in that row that comes first in ABC order. Underline the picture that comes last in each line.

hat	coat	mittens	bike
duck	bird	lion	cat
ball	glove	cap	shirt
tree	grass	bush	leaf

Name: _____

Alphabetizing

Directions: Look at each row of words. There is a line by each word. Write 1, 2, 3 or 4 to show where it should be in ABC order.

Example:

1. __1__ bell   __4__ well   __2__ smell   __3__ tell

2. ____ bite   ____ kite   ____ write   ____ might

3. ____ tar   ____ car   ____ far   ____ bar

4. ____ sand   ____ land   ____ band   ____ fanned

5. ____ sweet   ____ meat   ____ eat   ____ treat

6. ____ hair   ____ pear   ____ tear   ____ wear

7. ____ lake   ____ bake   ____ rake   ____ take

8. ____ round   ____ sound   ____ pound   ____ found

Name: _____

Alphabetizing

Directions: Put each row of words in ABC order. If the first letters of two words are the same, look at the next letters.

Example:

1. __1__ candy   __2__ carrot   __4__ duck   __3__ dance

2. ____ cold   ____ hot   ____ carry   ____ hit

3. ____ flash   ____ fan   ____ fun   ____ garden

4. ____ seat   ____ sun   ____ saw   ____ sit

5. ____ row   ____ ring   ____ rock   ____ run

6. ____ truck   ____ turn   ____ twin   ____ talk

7. ____ seven   ____ shoe   ____ soup   ____ smell

8. ____ pay   ____ penny   ____ pocket   ____ plant

Name: _____

Review

Directions: Read each question and follow the instructions.

1. Look at the picture. Now put the story in order. Write 1, 2, 3 or 4 on the line before each sentence.

Dad Drops Dinner

____ Dad cooks the meat.

____ Dad puts on his big hat.

____ The meat falls on the ground.

____ Dad cooks more meat.

2. Look at the words in each row across. Put them in ABC order. Circle the word that is first. Underline the word that is second. Box the word that is last.

dog	march	walk
hide	hit	game
make	men	moon
no	name	need
sea	sun	shovel

Name: _____

Finding Antonyms

Antonyms are words that are opposites. Example: hot, cold.
Directions: Draw a line from the word on the left to its antonym on the right.

sad	white
bottom	stop
black	fat
tall	top
thin	hard
little	found
cold	short
lost	hot
go	big
soft	happy

Name: _____

Finding Antonyms

Dapper Dog is going on a trip.

Directions: Use the crossword puzzle to find where he is going. Write the antonym of each clue.

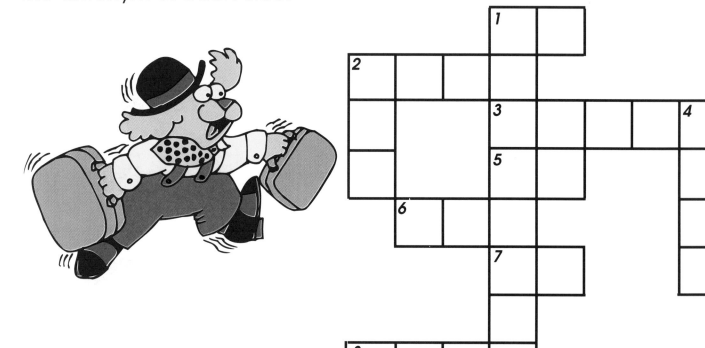

Across:
1. stop
2. under
3. behind
5. yes
6. good
7. pa
8. hit

Down:
1. grandpa's
2. in
4. light

Dapper's answer is hidden in 1 down. Where is he going?

_____

_____

_____

Name: _____

Finding Antonyms

Directions: Look at the picture. Read the sentences below it. Finish each sentence with the right antonym. A clue is given beside each sentence. Color the picture.

1. Dapper's suitcase is
   (Antonym for **closed**.)

   _____ .

2. Dapper has a ___ on his face.
   (Antonym for **frown**.)

   _____ .

3. His pillow is
   (Antonym for **hard**.)

   _____ .

4. Dapper's coat is
   (Antonym for **little**.)

   _____ .

5. He packs his stuffed animal
   (Antonym for **first**.)

   _____ .

Name: _____

Finding Homonyms

Homonyms sound the same but are spelled differently. They have different meanings, too. Sometimes homonyms can be more than two words.

Example: to, too, two. These are three words that sound the same.

Directions: Draw a line from the word on the left to its homonym.

blue	knight
night	too
beet	blew
write	see
hi	meet
two	son
meat	bee
sea	high
be	right
sun	beat

Name: _____

Finding Homonyms

Directions: Look at each picture. Circle the homonym that is spelled the right way.

deer   dear

blue   blew

to   two

hi   high

by   bye

new   knew

ate   eight

red   read

Name: _____

Finding Homonyms

Directions: Jane is having a birthday party. Complete each sentence with a homonym from the word box. Then write the word in the puzzle.

blew   son
blue   two
too   to
sun   write
right   bee
be   knew
new

Across:

1. Jane _____ on the candles.
4. Two days ago she was stung by a _____.
5. But after _____ days she feels better.

Down:

1. She has on a _____ dress for her party.
2. She will _____ a letter to her grandma.
3. Jane is a girl, so she is not a _____.

Finding Homonyms

Directions: Look at the word. Circle the picture that goes with the word.

1. sun

2. hi

3. ate

4. four

5. buy

6. hear

Review

Directions: Look at each question. Follow the instructions.

1. Draw a line from the word on the left to its antonym on the right.

high	down
in	you
big	low
up	little
me	out

2. Look at each picture. Circle the right word.

here   hear

know   no

3. Look at each word. Write its homonym beside it.

right _____   new _____

blew _____   dear _____

Tracking

Tom and Tess walk to school together each day. After school they stop at the park to play. Then they go home.

Directions: Look at the map. Use an orange crayon to show Tom's path. He starts at his home. Then he goes to school. When he leaves school he stops at the park. Then he goes home.

Use a blue crayon to show Tess's path. She goes the same places that Tom goes. Some of their paths will be the same.

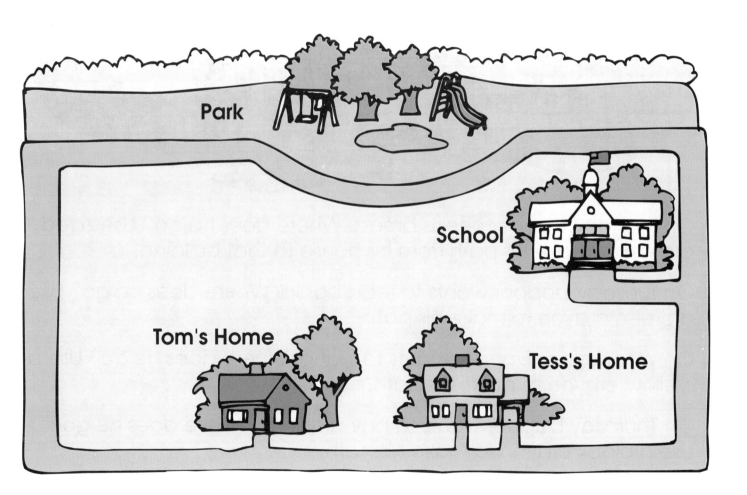

Name: _____

Tracking

Every morning Dapper wakes up and has to go somewhere. Where does he go?

Directions: Look at the map and follow the instructions.

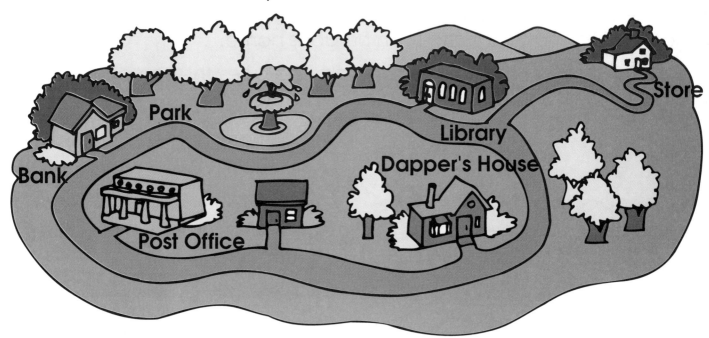

1. On Monday Dapper needs bread. Where does he go? Use a red crayon to make his path from his house to that building.

2. On Tuesday Dapper wants to read books. Where does he go? Use a green crayon to make his path.

3. On Wednesday Dapper wants to swing. Where does he go? Use a yellow crayon to make his path.

4. On Thursday Dapper wants to buy a stamp. Where does he go? Use a black crayon to make his path.

5. On Friday Dapper wants to get money. Where does he go? Use a purple crayon to make his path.

Name: _____

Tracking

Directions: Look at the path Dapper Dog took on page 44 . On this page, number in order 1 to 5 the places Dapper went on Monday, Tuesday, Wednesday, Thursday and Friday. Write the number, 1, 2, 3, 4 or 5 beside the name of the correct building.

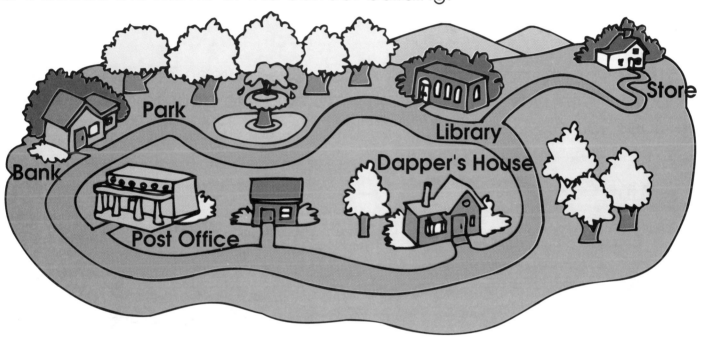

_____ Post Office

_____ Park

_____ Store

_____ Bank

_____ Library

Name: _____

Tracking

One day Tess had to go to the library after school. She didn't walk home with Tom.

Directions: Use a pink crayon to show Tess's path. She leaves her house in the morning to go to school. She goes to the library after school. Then she goes home.

Tom does not to go to the park today. Use a green crayon to show his path. He leaves his house in the morning. He goes to school. Then he goes home.

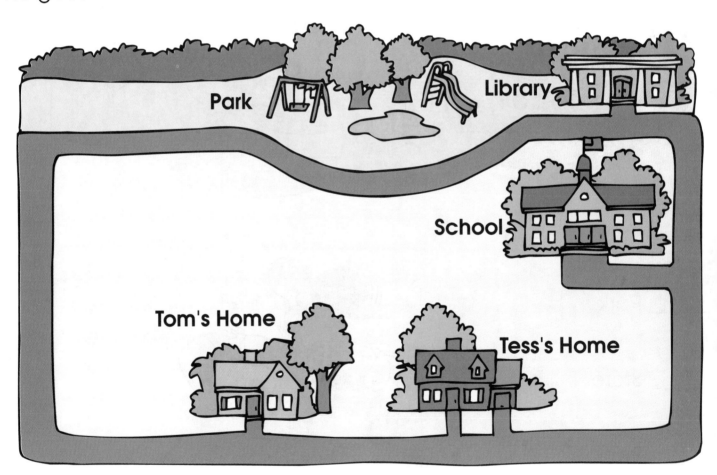

Name: _____

Tracking

Directions: Look at the map of the United States and follow the instructions.

1. Put a star in the state where you live.
2. Draw a line from your state to the Atlantic Ocean.
3. Put a triangle in the Atlantic Ocean.
4. Put a circle in the Pacific Ocean.
5. Color each state a different color.

Name: _____

Tracking

Tess's kitten, Sandy, is missing. Tess thinks she may have climbed into a tree.

Directions: Start at Tess's house. Use a green crayon to draw a path from her house to each tree on the map.

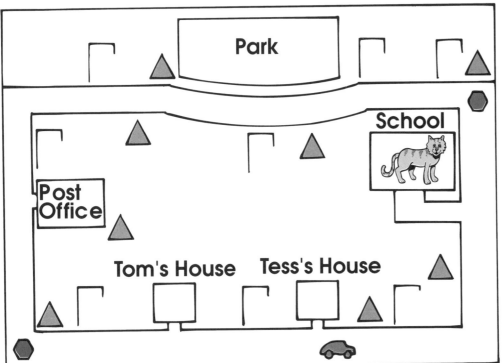

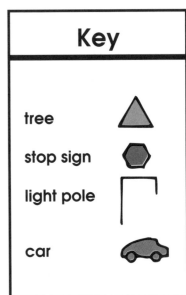

1. Tom thinks Sandy may have climbed a light pole. Use a black crayon to draw a path from Tom's house to each light pole.
2. Tess's mother says she will drive the car around and look for Sandy. Use a red crayon to make her path on every street. Put an **X** every time Tess's mother has to stop at a red light or a stop sign.
3. Now look at the map very closely. Do you see Sandy? Put a purple line from Tess to her kitten.

Where was Sandy? _____

_____

Name: _____

Tracking

Directions: Look at Dapper's home. Look at the paths he takes to the oven and the back door. The small numbers on each path show how many steps Dapper must take to get there. Now follow the instructions.

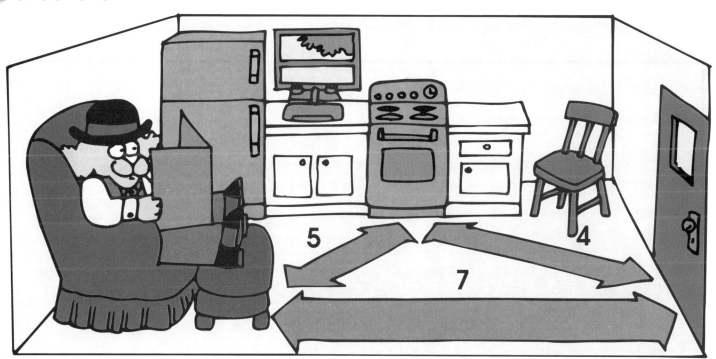

1. Dapper's cookies are done. Use a black crayon to trace Dapper's path from his chair to the oven. How many steps does Dapper take?_____

2. While Dapper is looking in his oven, he hears a noise in the back yard. Use the black crayon to show Dapper's path. How many steps has Dapper taken in all?_____

3. Now Dapper is going back to his chair. How many steps must he take?_____ How many steps has he taken in all? _____

4. Dapper's path has made a shape. What shape is it?_____

Name: _____

Review

Directions: Use the space below to draw a map of your neighborhood - - or any neighborhood. On your map, draw a school, a library, a home and a store. Then mark a path that tracks a path from (1) home to (2) school to (3) library to (4) store to (5) home.

Predicting Outcome

Directions: Read the story. Finish the last box. What will Jane do? What will she say?

1. "Do you want to go to the library with me?"
   "Yes, I want a book about seashells."

2. "Good. Here is my book about space ships."

3. "Have you found your book?"
   "No. I can't find it."
   "Why don't you ask someone?"

4. What do you think Jane will do?

Name: _____

Predicting Outcome

Directions: Read the story. Use the last box to finish it.

1. "Look at that elephant! He sure is big!"

2. "I'm hungry."
   "I bet that elephant is, too."

3. "Stop, Tess! Look at that sign!"

4. What will Tom and Tess do?

Predicting Outcome

Directions: Read the story. Finish the story the way you think it should end. Then color your picture.

1. A cat is playing with a ball of yarn.

2. A mouse begins peeking around the corner.

3. The mouse tiptoes past the playful cat.

4. What do you think will happen?

Name: _____

Making Inferences

Directions: Read the story. Answer the questions.

Mrs. Posey is looking forward to a visit from Grandma Dapper. That morning, she cleans her house. She bakes a cherry pie. An hour before Grandma Dapper is to arrive, the phone rings. Mrs. Posey says she understands. But she looks very sad.

1. Who do you think called Mrs. Posey?

_____

_____

2. Why?

_____

_____

3. Why is Mrs. Posey sad?

_____

_____

_____

Name: _____

Making Inferences

Directions: Read the story. Follow the instructions.

John and his Dad are going to a baseball game today. The game starts at 2:00 p.m. John wakes up at 9:00 a.m. He has a swimming class at 10:30. His class is over at 11:30 a.m. John has lunch at noon. Then he must clean his room. Dad says, "We must leave at 1:30." But John wants to play with his friend, too. Dad says, "Play after you clean your room, but before we leave for the game."

1. Use a black crayon to draw game time on the clock.
2. Use a red crayon to draw when swimming class starts.
3. How long is swimming class?_____
4. Use an orange crayon to draw lunch time on the clock.
5. What does John do right after lunch? _____

_____

_____

6. How much time do you think John will have to play?

_____

_____

7. Use a blue crayon to draw the time when John and his Dad must leave for the game.

Name: _____

Making Inferences

Directions: Read the story. Then answer the questions.

Tom is baking cookies. He wears special clothes when he bakes. He puts flour, sugar, eggs and butter into a bowl. He mixes everything together. He puts them in the oven at 11:15 a.m. It takes them 15 minutes to bake. Tom wants something cold and white to drink when he eats his cookies.

1. Tom is baking a cake.   **True** or **False** (Circle one.)

2. Tom wears a (**hat mittens apron tie**) when he bakes. (Circle two.)

3. Cross out the thing that Tom does not put in the cookies.

      flour   eggs   milk   butter   sugar

4. What do you think Tom does after he mixes the cookies, but before he bakes them?

_____

_____

5. What time will the cookies be done? _____

6. What will Tom drink with his cookies?_____

7. Why do you think Tom wanted to bake cookies?

_____

_____

_____

Making Inferences

Directions: Read the story. Answer the questions.

Jane and her family are on a trip. It is very sunny. Jane loves to swim. She also likes the waves. But there is something else she likes even more. Jane builds drip castles. She makes drips by using very wet sand. She lets it drip out of her hand into a tall pile. She makes the drip piles as high as she can.

1. Where is Jane? _____

_____

2. What does Jane wear on her trip? _____

_____

3. Is Jane **hot** or **cold?** (circle one) _____

_____

4. What does Jane like to do best? _____

_____

5. What are drip castles made from? _____

_____

6. What do you think happens when drip castles get too big? _____

_____

7. If Jane gets too hot, what do you think she does? _____

Name: _____

Review

Directions: Look at each question. Follow the instructions.

A. Dapper Dog is boating.

B. He likes small waves.

C. That boat makes the waves big.

D. What do you think will happen?

Tess is going to her softball game.
The game starts after school.
Tess is the pitcher and her friend,
Sue, is the catcher.

1. Does the game start in the **morning** or **afternoon**? (Circle one.)

2. Does Tess wear **sandals** or **gym shoes**? (Circle one.)

3. What does Tess wear on her hand
   at the game?   _____

4. Who does Tess throw the ball to? _____

Name: _____

Learning Dictionary Skills

A dictionary tells you many things. It tells you what words mean. It tells you how words sound.

Words in a dictionary are in ABC order. That makes them easier to find.

A picture dictionary lists a word, its picture and its meaning. All the words on this page start with the letter **B**. Look at this picture dictionary. Then answer the questions.

baby

A very young child.

band

A group of people who play music.

bank

A place where money is kept.

---

bark

The sound a dog makes.

berry

A small, juicy fruit.

board

A flat piece of wood.

---

1. What is a small, juicy fruit? _____

2. What is a group of people who play music? _____

3. The name for a very young child is a _____ .

4. A flat piece of wood is called a _____ .

Name: _____

Learning Dictionary Skills

Directions: Read the picture dictionary. Then use it to answer the questions.

safe	**sea**	**seed**

A metal box.	A body of water.	The beginning of a plant.

sheep	**shop**	**skate**

An animal that has wool.	A store.	A shoe that has wheels or a blade on it.

snowstorm	**squirrel**	**stone**

A time when a lot of snow falls.	A small animal with a bushy tail.	A small rock.

1. What kind of animal has wool? _____

2. What do you call a shoe with wheels on it? _____

3. When a lot of snow falls it is called a _____ .

4. A small animal with a bushy tail is called a _____ .

5. Another name for a store is a _____ .

6. A plant starts as a _____ .

Name: _____

Learning Dictionary Skills

Directions: Look at the **guide words** in bold on this page. Then look at the words that come between the **guide words**. Answer the questions.

table   **tiger**

table	**tail**	**teacher**

Furniture with legs and a flat top.	A slender part that is on the back of an animal.	A person who teaches lessons.

telephone	**ticket**	**tiger**
	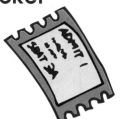	
Something that sends and receives sounds.	A paper slip or card.	An animal that has stripes.

1. What are the guide words on this page? _____ and _____
2. Who is a person who teaches lessons? _____
3. Name an animal with stripes. _____
4. What is a piece of furniture with legs and a flat top? _____
5. A paper card or slip is a _____.
6. The part on the back of an animal is a _____.

Name: _____

Learning Dictionary Skills

Directions: Look at the two dictionary pages. What are their guide words? Put each word from the word box in ABC order between each pair of guide words.

face	**field**	**fierce**	**flat**

fix	faint	fire	fit	flush
flash	fan	far	farm	family
finish	farmer	fast	fat	fill
farther	feed	first	feel	fail
fence	few	fight	flag	fish

Learning Dictionary Skills

Some words have more than one meaning. A dictionary numbers each meaning.

Directions: Read the meanings of **tag**. Then follow the instructions.

tag —
1. A small strip or tab attached to something else.
2. To label.
3. To follow closely and constantly.
4. A game of chase.

Read each sentence. Write the number of the correct definition.

1. We will play a game of tag after we study.   _____

2. I will tag this coat with its price.   _____

3. My little brother will tag along with us.   _____

4. My mother already took off the price tag.   _____

5. The tag on the puppy said, "For Sale."   _____

6. Do not tag that tree.   _____

Review

Directions: Read each question. Follow the instructions.

1. Circle the picture that comes first in the dictionary.

Indian

neighbor

seed

2. Circle the sentences that describe **guide words**.
   A. They are the first and the last words on a dictionary page.
   B. They are also written at the top of the page.
   C. They help you find words in a dictionary.
   D. They are hard to see on the page.

3. Read the meanings of **print**. Answer the question.

   print —   1. To stamp onto a surface.
             2. To offer in printed form.
             3. To write with letters separated.

   Write the definition of print that best fits this sentence:
   Please **print** your name carefully on the page.

   _____

   _____

   _____

4. Look at the meaning of **bliss**. Now write a sentence using **bliss** in it.
   bliss — Very great happiness, joy.

   _____

   _____

   _____

Pretty As a Picture

You need a red crayon and a blue crayon.
Read the words in each part of the picture.
If the words have the same meaning, color the part RED.
If the words do not have the same meaning, color the part BLUE.

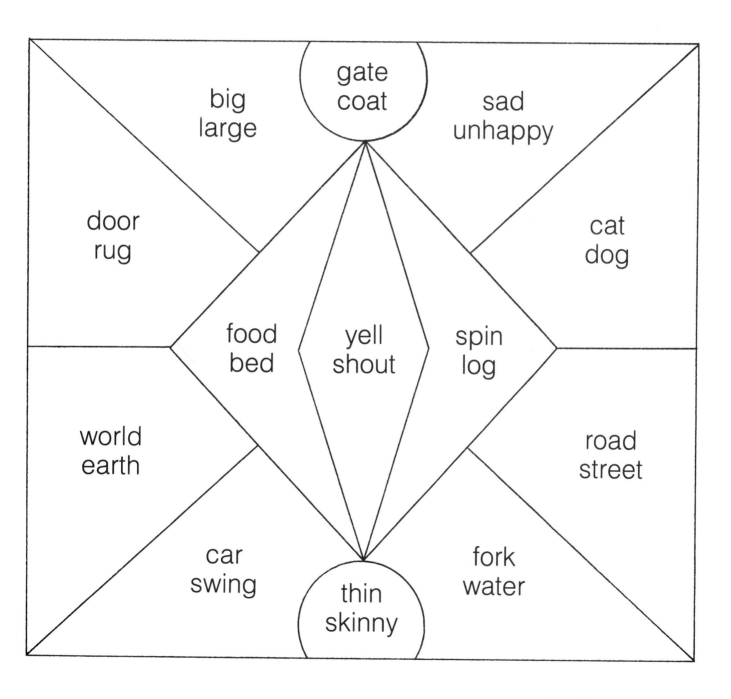

Find the Mistakes

Here is Benny's homework paper.
Benny had to read each word on the paper.
He had to write a word that means the opposite.
Poor Benny, he made a lot of mistakes.
Correct his paper.
Mark ✓ next to each right answer.
Mark X next to each wrong answer.
For each wrong answer, change Benny's word.
Write a word that means the opposite of the word on the paper.

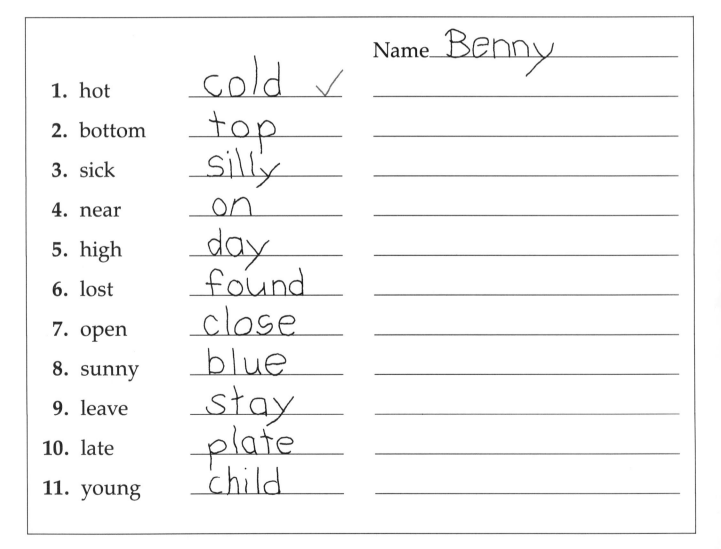

Name Benny

1. hot — cold ✓ _____

2. bottom — top _____

3. sick — silly _____

4. near — on _____

5. high — day _____

6. lost — found _____

7. open — close _____

8. sunny — blue _____

9. leave — stay _____

10. late — plate _____

11. young — child _____

Identifying and writing antonyms

The Long Sneeze

A person once sneezed for 150 days without stopping.

You can find out if this is true.
Look at the box filled with words.
You see each word 2 times.

bat	left	can	fan	rest	yard
bat	left	can	fan	rest	yard

Now read the sentences below.
Write a word from the box to finish each sentence.
Cross out each word after you use it.
When you are done, a word in the box will not be crossed out.
If that word has 4 letters, the sneeze story is true.
If that word has 3 letters, the sneeze story is not true.

It is hot. Turn on the _____.

I need my baseball _____.

The car must turn _____.

How many apples are _____

on the plate?

Where are the _____ of my

toys?

Open a _____ of beans.

I _____ buy that robot.

I need a _____ of rope.

I worked hard and need to

_____.

I am a rock-and-roll _____.

A _____ lives in a cave.

Which word was not crossed out? _____

Is the sneeze story true? _____

Using multiple meaning words

Riddle-De-Day

Try to make a grown-up laugh.
Read each riddle.
If your grown-up laughs, circle YES.
If your grown-up does not laugh, circle NO.

1. Question: Why is a river rich?

    Answer: Because it has two banks.　　　　　YES　　　NO

2. Question: Why is the cook mean?

    Answer: Because he beats the eggs and whips
    　　　　　the cream.　　　　　YES　　　NO

3. Question: What did the rug say to the floor?

    Answer: Stick 'em up. I've got you covered.　　　YES　　　NO

4. Question: What has 18 legs and catches flies?

    Answer: A baseball team.　　　　　YES　　　NO

5. Question: When is a piece of wood like a king?

    Answer: When it is a ruler.　　　　　YES　　　NO

6. Question: What part of the fish weighs the
    　　　　　most?

    Answer: The scales.　　　　　YES　　　NO

7. Question: Why did the basketball need a bib?

    Answer: Because it dribbled.　　　　　YES　　　NO

8. Question: What has a head, a tail, but no body?

    Answer: A penny.　　　　　YES　　　NO

Vacation Time

It is vacation time.
Some children are going away.
Jill is going skiing.
Paul is going to the seashore.
Ana is going to Washington, D.C.

Each child has a suitcase.
Each suitcase is packed.
Figure out who gets each suitcase.
Circle the right name.

Jill   Paul   Ana

Jill   Paul   Ana

Jill   Paul   Ana

Pack a suitcase for a trip to
a cabin in the woods.
Write 3 things you will need.

_____

_____

_____

Identifying objects in categories; drawing conclusions

It's a Problem

Mike has a problem.

What will Mike do now?
Write your idea.

_____

_____

_____

_____

_____

_____

Learning to predict outcomes

Birthday Party

Plan a birthday party.
You may invite 4 friends.
Write their names.

_____

_____

_____

_____

Decide on 4 special things to do for the party.
You may go bowling, go to the movies, invite
a magician, whatever you want.

First we will _____

_____

Second we will _____

_____

Third we will _____

_____

Fourth we will _____

_____

You will be given birthday gifts.
Write down 4 gifts you would like to have.

_____   _____

_____   _____

Sequencing events

Off to the Movies

Here is a movie poster.
It is filled with information.
Read the poster and then answer the questions.

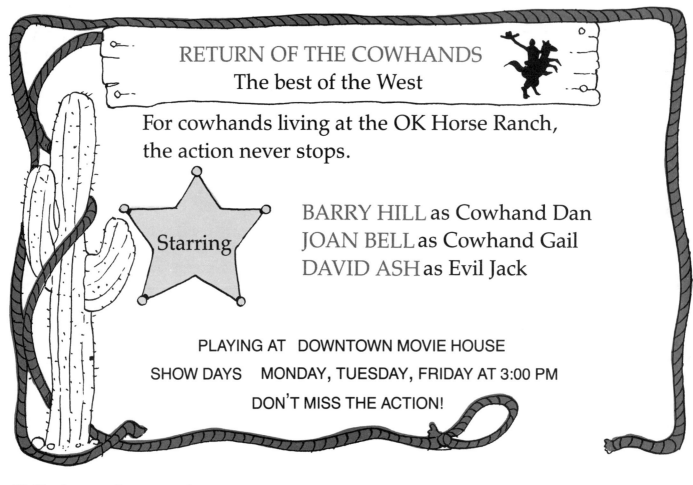

RETURN OF THE COWHANDS
The best of the West

For cowhands living at the OK Horse Ranch,
the action never stops.

Starring

BARRY HILL as Cowhand Dan
JOAN BELL as Cowhand Gail
DAVID ASH as Evil Jack

PLAYING AT   DOWNTOWN MOVIE HOUSE

SHOW DAYS   MONDAY, TUESDAY, FRIDAY AT 3:00 PM

DON'T MISS THE ACTION!

Tell about the movie.

What is the name of the movie? _____

Who plays Evil Jack? _____

Where do the cowhands live? _____

Can you see the show on Sunday? _____

What time is the show? _____

ANSWER KEY

MASTER THINKING SKILLS
2

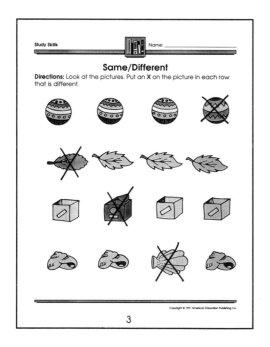

Same/Different

Dapper Dog wants a new house. Help him find the shapes he needs.

Directions: Look at Dapper Dog's old house. Now look at the boxes of shapes. Which box has all the same shapes in it? Color those shapes.

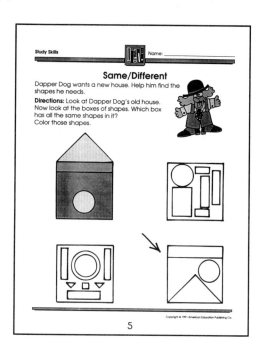

5

Making Deductions

Tom and Tess are looking for gold. They have found many shapes. Which one has the gold in it?

Directions: Look at the shapes. Then answer the questions.

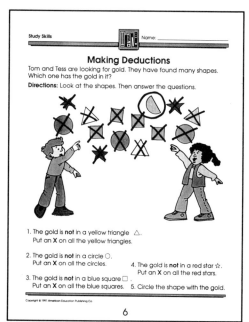

1. The gold is **not** in a yellow triangle △.
   Put an **X** on all the yellow triangles.

2. The gold is **not** in a circle ○.
   Put an **X** on all the circles.

3. The gold is **not** in a blue square □.
   Put an **X** on all the blue squares.

4. The gold is **not** in a red star ☆.
   Put an **X** on all the red stars.

5. Circle the shape with the gold.

6

Making Deductions

Now Tom and Tess are late for dinner. What time is dinner?

Directions: Look at the clock. Then answer the questions.

1. It is now 6:00 p.m. Use an orange crayon for the clock's hands.

2. It was 3:00 when they left home. Draw the clock hands in blue.

3. Mother said, "Dinner is in two hours. Be home then." Draw the clock hands in purple.

4. What time were they to be home? __5:00__

7

Making Deductions

Dad is cooking dinner tonight.

Directions: Look at the clues below. Fill in the menu. What day is it?

Menu	
Monday	pizza
Tuesday	chicken
Wednesday	corn
Thursday	meat pie
Friday	hot dogs
Saturday	fish
Sunday	cheese rolls

1. Mom fixed pizza on Monday.

2. Dad fixed cheese rolls the day before that.

3. Tess made meat pie three days after Mom fixed pizza.

4. Tom fixed corn-on-the-cob the day before Tess made meat pie.

5. Mom fixed hotdogs the day after Tess made meat pie.

6. Tess cooked fish the day before Dad fixed cheese rolls.

7. Dad is making chicken today. What day is it? __Tuesday__

8

Making Deductions

Directions: Use the clues to help the children find their books. Draw a line from each child's name to the right book.

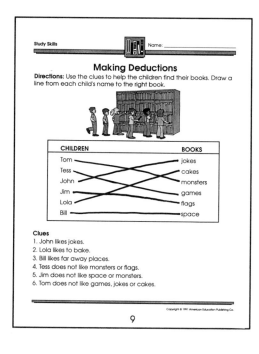

CHILDREN	BOOKS
Tom	jokes
Tess	cakes
John	monsters
Jim	games
Lola	flags
Bill	space

Clues
1. John likes jokes.
2. Lola likes to bake.
3. Bill likes far away places.
4. Tess does not like monsters or flags.
5. Jim does not like space or monsters.
6. Tom does not like games, jokes or cakes.

9

Review

Directions: Look at each question. Follow the instructions.

1. Circle the box of shapes that matches Dapper's.

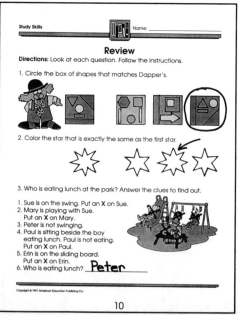

2. Color the star that is exactly the same as the first star.

3. Who is eating lunch at the park? Answer the clues to find out.

1. Sue is on the swing. Put an **X** on Sue.
2. Mary is playing with Sue. Put an **X** on Mary.
3. Peter is not swinging.
4. Paul is sitting beside the boy eating lunch. Paul is not eating. Put an **X** on Paul.
5. Erin is on the sliding board. Put an **X** on Erin.
6. Who is eating lunch? __Peter__

10

74

Classifying

Directions: Look at each leaf and read each leaf's name. Then follow the instructions.

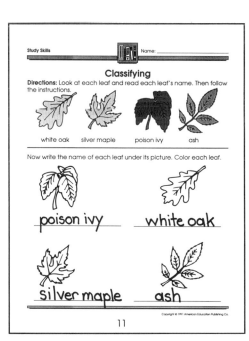

white oak   silver maple   poison ivy   ash

Now write the name of each leaf under its picture. Color each leaf.

poison ivy   white oak

silver maple   ash

11

Classifying

Directions: Go outside and find some leaves. Put your leaves into groups. Do you know their names?

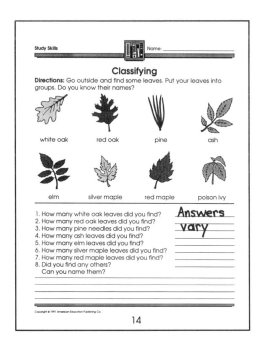

white oak   red oak   pine   ash

elm   silver maple   red maple   poison ivy

1. How many white oak leaves did you find?
2. How many red oak leaves did you find?
3. How many pine needles did you find?
4. How many ash leaves did you find?
5. How many elm leaves did you find?
6. How many silver maple leaves did you find?
7. How many red maple leaves did you find?
8. Did you find any others?
   Can you name them?

Answers vary

14

Classifying

Directions: Look closely at the tricky tree. It has four different kinds of leaves: ash, poison ivy, silver maple and white oak. Then follow the instructions.

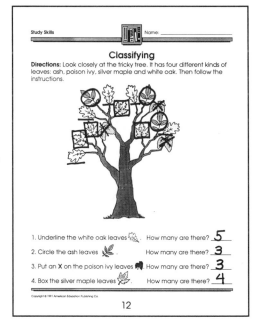

1. Underline the white oak leaves. How many are there? **5**

2. Circle the ash leaves. How many are there? **3**

3. Put an **X** on the poison ivy leaves. How many are there? **3**

4. Box the silver maple leaves. How many are there? **4**

12

Classifying

Directions: Circle the things on the menu that Dapper Dog will eat. He likes fruit and things made from fruit. He likes bread.

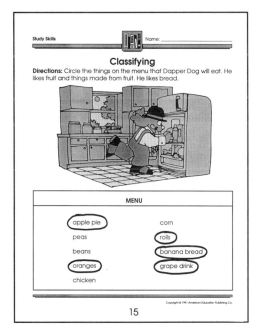

MENU

apple pie   corn

peas   rolls

beans   banana bread

oranges   grape drink

chicken

15

Classifying

Poison ivy is not safe. If you touch it, it can make your skin red and itchy. It can hurt. It grows on the ground. It has three leaves. It can be green or red.

Directions: Watch out Dapper Dog! There is poison ivy in these woods. Color the poison ivy leaves red. Then color the other "safe" leaves other colors.

R = color red, poison ivy.

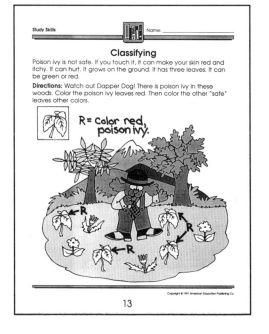

13

Classifying

Directions: Use a red crayon to circle the names of 3 animals you would want for a pet. Use a blue crayon to circle the names of 3 wild animals. Use an orange crayon to circle the 2 animals that are pests.

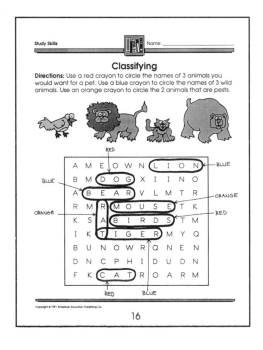

```
A M E O W N  L I O N   BLUE
B M D O G X I I N O
A B E A R V L M T R   ORANGE
R M R M O U S E T K   RED
K S A B I R D S M Y
I K T I G E R M Y Q
B U N O W R Q N E N
D N C P H I D U D N
F K C A T R O A R M
```

RED   BLUE

16

75

Classifying

Dapper Dog is going on a camping trip.

Directions: Put an **X** on the word in each row across that does not belong in that group.

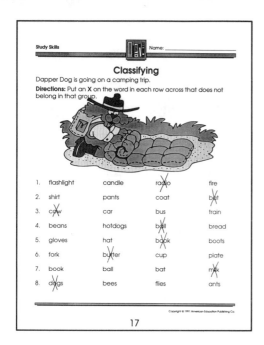

1.	flashlight	candle	radio	fire
2.	shirt	pants	coat	bat
3.	cow	car	bus	train
4.	beans	hotdogs	ball	bread
5.	gloves	hat	book	boots
6.	fork	butter	cup	plate
7.	book	ball	bat	milk
8.	dogs	bees	flies	ants

17

Review

Directions: Follow the instructions for each question.

1. Look at the leaf on the left. Now look at the pictures of the other 3 leaves. Write the missing name under the leaf.

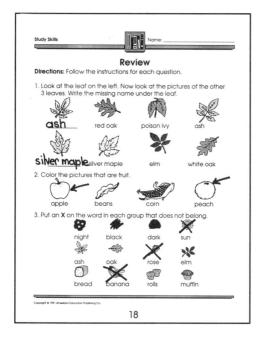

2. Color the pictures that are fruit.

3. Put an **X** on the word in each group that does not belong.

18

Finding Patterns

Directions: Finish each row with the right shape.

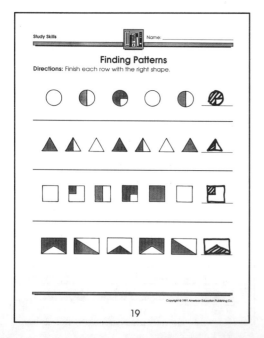

19

Finding Patterns

Directions: Look at each shape. Use a crayon to trace the shape of any letter you see inside it.

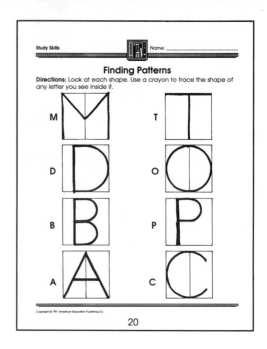

20

Finding Patterns

Directions: Look at the box on the left. Find the box on the right that has the same pattern of shades in it. Draw a line between the two.

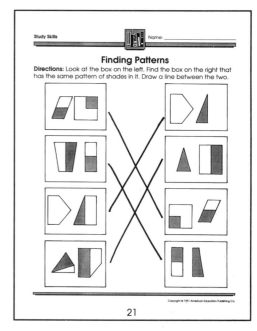

21

Finding Analogies

Example:

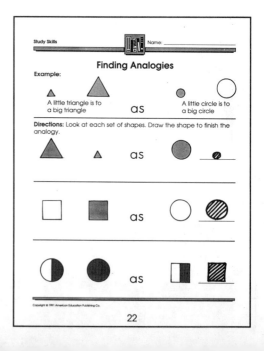

Directions: Look at each set of shapes. Draw the shape to finish the analogy.

22

Finding Analogies

Directions: Look at the shapes. Draw the shape that finishes the analogy.

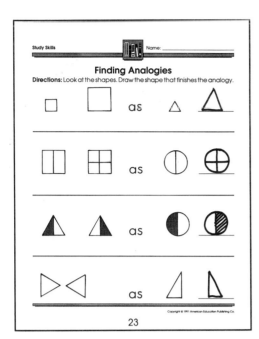

23

Finding Analogies

Directions: Look at the shapes on the left. Find the shapes that finish the analogy on the right. Draw a line between them.

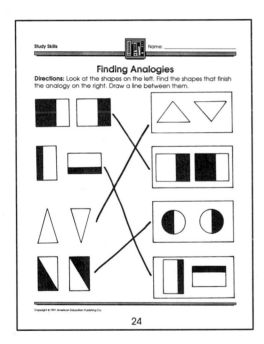

24

Finding Analogies

Directions: Look at the shapes on the left. Draw two shapes to complete the analogy.

Answers vary, samples:

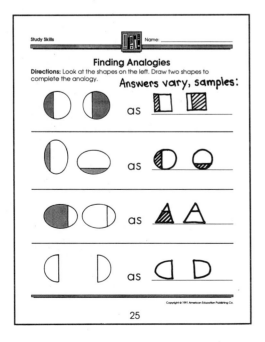

25

Review

Directions: Look at each question. Follow the instructions.

1. Trace **M** as many times as you can find it.

2. Complete the pattern in the last square.

3. Look at the first three shapes. Draw a shape that completes the analogy.

4. Make an analogy to the shapes below.   Answer varies

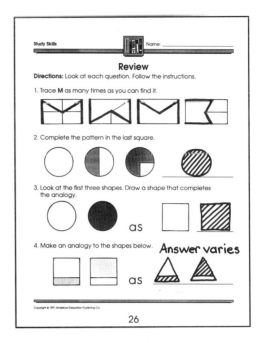

26

Sequencing

Tom and Tess are making a snack. They are fixing nacho chips and cheese.

Directions: Look at the picture. Then look at the steps that Tom and Tess use. They are all mixed up. Help Tom and Tess decide what to do first. Put the numbers beside each sentence to tell them which steps come first. Then color the picture.

5 Tom and Tess cook the chips in the oven for 2 minutes.
2 They get out a plate to cook on.
1 Tom and Tess get out the nacho chips and cheese.
6 Tom and Tess eat the food.
3 They put the chips on a plate.
4 They put cheese on the chips.

27

Sequencing

Directions: Kate is sick. What to you think happened? Put numbers beside each sentence to tell the story.

2 She went to the doctor's office.
9 Kate felt much better.
1 Kate felt very hot and tired.
6 Kate's mother went to the drug store.
4 The doctor wrote down something.
3 The doctor looked in Kate's ears.
7 Kate took a pill.
5 The doctor gave Kate's mother the piece of paper.
8 Kate drank some water with her pill.

28

Sequencing

Directions: Dapper Dog wants to make a new friend today. Help him by putting in order the steps for meeting the little boy in the picture.

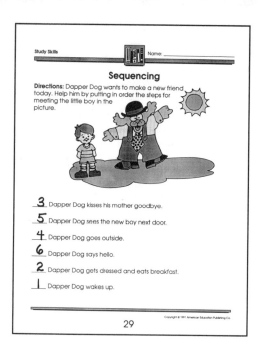

__3__ Dapper Dog kisses his mother goodbye.

__5__ Dapper Dog sees the new boy next door.

__4__ Dapper Dog goes outside.

__6__ Dapper Dog says hello.

__2__ Dapper Dog gets dressed and eats breakfast.

__1__ Dapper Dog wakes up.

29

Sequencing

Mrs. Posey is making a new hat.

Directions: Mrs. Posey has her story all mixed up. Read her story. Now on the lines below write the story in the order that you think it happened. Color the picture.

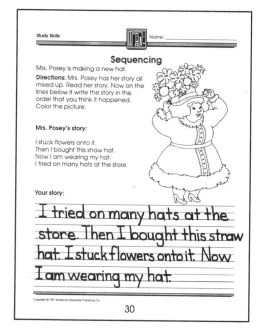

Mrs. Posey's story:

I stuck flowers onto it.
Then I bought this straw hat.
Now I am wearing my hat.
I tried on many hats at the store.

Your story:

I tried on many hats at the store. Then I bought this straw hat. I stuck flowers onto it. Now I am wearing my hat.

30

Alphabetizing

Sometimes words are put into ABC order. That means that if a word starts with A, it comes first. If it starts with B, it comes next, etc.

Directions: Look at each row of pictures. Circle the picture in that row that comes first in ABC order. Underline the picture that comes last in each line.

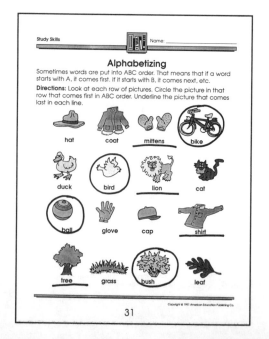

hat   coat   mittens   bike

duck   bird   lion   cat

ball   glove   cap   shirt

tree   grass   bush   leaf

31

Alphabetizing

Directions: Look at each row of words. There is a line by each word. Write 1, 2, 3 or 4 to show where it should be in ABC order.

Example:

1. __1__ bell   __4__ well   __2__ smell   __3__ tell
2. __1__ bite   __2__ kite   __4__ write   __3__ might
3. __4__ tar   __2__ car   __3__ far   __1__ bar
4. __4__ sand   __3__ land   __1__ band   __2__ fanned
5. __3__ sweet   __2__ meat   __1__ eat   __4__ treat
6. __1__ hair   __2__ pear   __3__ tear   __4__ wear
7. __2__ lake   __1__ bake   __3__ rake   __4__ take
8. __3__ round   __4__ sound   __2__ pound   __1__ found

32

Alphabetizing

Directions: Put each row of words in ABC order. If the first letters of two words are the same, look at the next letters.

Example:

1. __1__ candy   __2__ carrot   __4__ duck   __3__ dance
2. __2__ cold   __4__ hot   __1__ carry   __3__ hit
3. __2__ flash   __1__ fan   __3__ fun   __4__ garden
4. __2__ seat   __4__ sun   __1__ saw   __3__ sit
5. __3__ row   __1__ ring   __2__ rock   __4__ run
6. __2__ truck   __3__ turn   __4__ twin   __1__ talk
7. __1__ seven   __2__ shoe   __4__ soup   __3__ smell
8. __1__ pay   __2__ penny   __4__ pocket   __3__ plant

33

Review

Directions: Read each question and follow the instructions.

1. Look at the picture. Now put the story in order. Write 1, 2, 3 or 4 on the line before each sentence.

Dad Drops Dinner

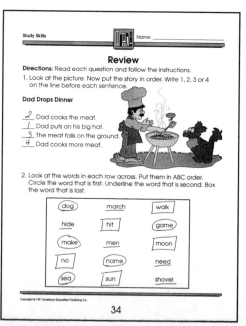

__2__ Dad cooks the meat.

__1__ Dad puts on his big hat.

__3__ The meat falls on the ground.

__4__ Dad cooks more meat.

2. Look at the words in each row across. Put them in ABC order. Circle the word that is first. Underline the word that is second. Box the word that is last.

dog	march	walk
hide	hit	game
make	men	moon
no	name	need
sea	sun	shovel

34

78

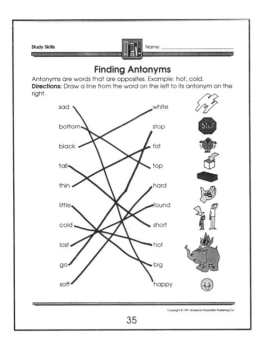

Study Skills   Name: _____

Finding Antonyms

Antonyms are words that are opposites. Example: hot, cold.

Directions: Draw a line from the word on the left to its antonym on the right.

sad	white
bottom	stop
black	fat
tall	top
thin	hard
little	found
cold	short
lost	hot
go	big
soft	happy

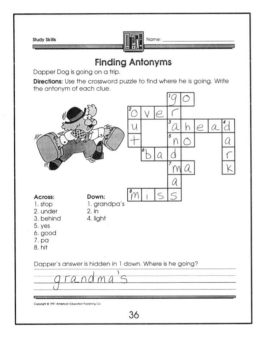

Study Skills   Name: _____

Finding Antonyms

Dapper Dog is going on a trip.

Directions: Use the crossword puzzle to find where he is going. Write the antonym of each clue.

Across:
1. stop
2. under
3. behind
5. yes
6. good
7. pa
8. hit

Down:
1. grandpa's
2. in
4. light

Dapper's answer is hidden in 1 down. Where is he going?

grandma's

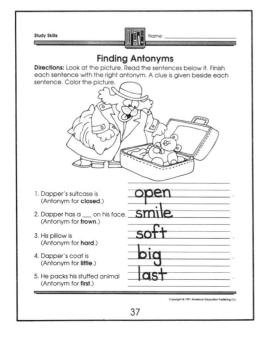

Study Skills   Name: _____

Finding Antonyms

Directions: Look at the picture. Read the sentences below it. Finish each sentence with the right antonym. A clue is given beside each sentence. Color the picture.

1. Dapper's suitcase is ____.   **open**
   (Antonym for **closed**.)
2. Dapper has a ___ on his face.   **smile**
   (Antonym for **frown**.)
3. His pillow is ____.   **soft**
   (Antonym for **hard**.)
4. Dapper's coat is ____.   **big**
   (Antonym for **little**.)
5. He packs his stuffed animal ____.   **last**
   (Antonym for **first**.)

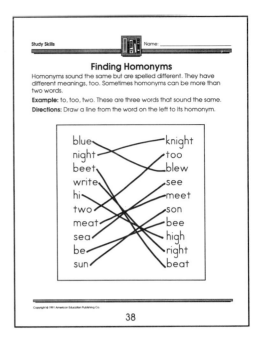

Study Skills   Name: _____

Finding Homonyms

Homonyms sound the same but are spelled different. They have different meanings, too. Sometimes homonyms can be more than two words.

Example: to, too, two. These are three words that sound the same.

Directions: Draw a line from the word on the left to its homonym.

blue	knight
night	too
beet	blew
write	see
hi	meet
two	son
meat	bee
sea	high
be	right
sun	beat

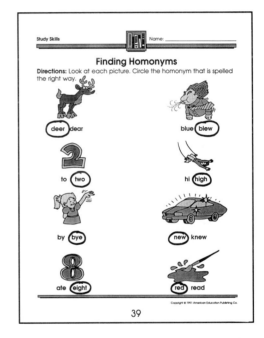

Study Skills   Name: _____

Finding Homonyms

Directions: Look at each picture. Circle the homonym that is spelled the right way.

deer   **dear**   blue   **blew**

to   **two**   hi   **high**

by   **bye**   **new**   knew

ate   **eight**   **red**   read

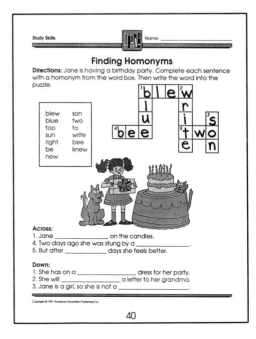

Study Skills   Name: _____

Finding Homonyms

Directions: Jane is having a birthday party. Complete each sentence with a homonym from the word box. Then write the word into the puzzle.

blew	son
blue	two
too	to
sun	write
right	bee
be	knew
new	

Across:
1. Jane _____ on the candles.
4. Two days ago she was stung by a _____.
5. But after _____ days she feels better.

Down:
1. She has on a _____ dress for her party.
2. She will _____ a letter to her grandma.
3. Jane is a girl, so she is not a _____.

Finding Homonyms

Directions: Look at the word. Circle the picture that goes with the word.

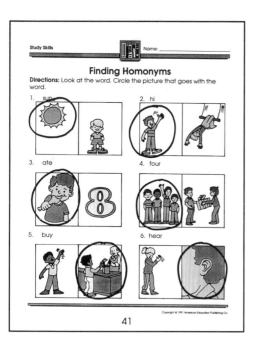

1. sun
2. hi
3. ate
4. four
5. buy
6. hear

41

Review

Directions: Look at each question. Follow the instructions.

1. Draw a line from the word on the left to its antonym on the right.

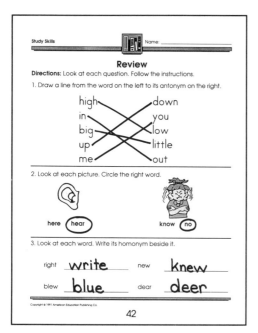

high — down
in — you
big — low
up — little
me — out

2. Look at each picture. Circle the right word.

here (hear)   know (no)

3. Look at each word. Write its homonym beside it.

right **write**   new **knew**

blew **blue**   dear **deer**

42

Tracking

Tom and Tess walk to school together each day. After school they stop at the park to play. Then they go home.

Directions: Look at the map. Use an orange crayon to show Tom's path. He starts at his home. Then he goes to school. When he leaves school he stops at the park. Then he goes home.

Use a blue crayon to show Tess's path. She goes the same places that Tom goes. Some of their paths will be the same.

43

Tracking

Every morning Dapper wakes up and has to go somewhere. Where does he go?

Directions: Look at the map and follow the instructions.

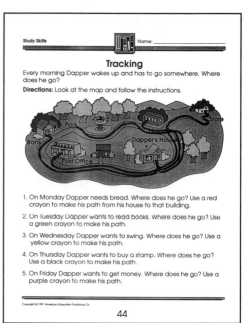

1. On Monday Dapper needs bread. Where does he go? Use a red crayon to make his path from his house to that building.

2. On Tuesday Dapper wants to read books. Where does he go? Use a green crayon to make his path.

3. On Wednesday Dapper wants to swing. Where does he go? Use a yellow crayon to make his path.

4. On Thursday Dapper wants to buy a stamp. Where does he go? Use a black crayon to make his path.

5. On Friday Dapper wants to get money. Where does he go? Use a purple crayon to make his path.

44

Tracking

Directions: Look at the path Dapper Dog took on page 42. On this page, number in order 1 to 5 the places Dapper went on Monday, Tuesday, Wednesday, Thursday and Friday. Write the number, 1, 2, 3, 4 or 5 beside the name of the correct building.

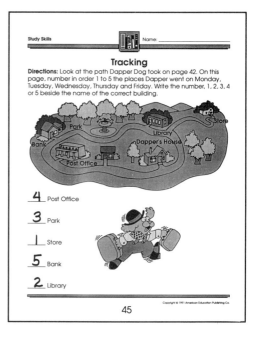

4 Post Office

3 Park

1 Store

5 Bank

2 Library

45

Tracking

One day Tess had to go to the library after school. She didn't walk home with Tom.

Directions: Use a pink crayon to show Tess's path. She leaves her house in the morning to go to school. She goes to the library after school. Then she goes home.

Tom does not go to the park today. Use a green crayon to show his path. He leaves his house in the morning. He goes to school. Then he goes home.

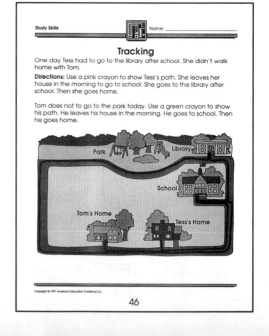

46

Tracking

Directions: Look at the map of the United States and follow the instructions.

1. Put a star in the state where you live.
2. Draw a line from your state to the Atlantic Ocean.
3. Put a triangle in the Atlantic Ocean.
4. Put a circle in the Pacific Ocean.
5. Color each state a different color.

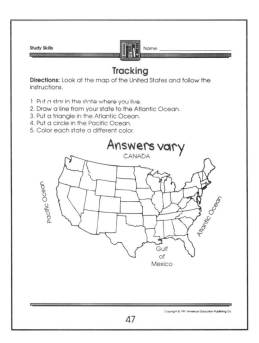

Answers vary

Tracking

Tess's kitten, Sandy, is missing. Tess thinks she may have climbed into a tree.

Directions: Start at Tess's house. Use a green crayon to draw a path from her house to each tree on the map.

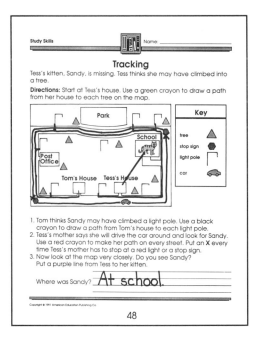

1. Tom thinks Sandy may have climbed a light pole. Use a black crayon to draw a path from Tom's house to each light pole.
2. Tess's mother says she will drive the car around and look for Sandy. Use a red crayon to make her path on every street. Put an **X** every time Tess's mother has to stop at a red light or a stop sign.
3. Now look at the map very closely. Do you see Sandy? Put a purple line from Tess to her kitten.

Where was Sandy? **At school.**

Tracking

Directions: Look at Dapper's home. Look at the paths he takes to the oven and the back door. The small numbers on each path show how many steps Dapper must take to get there. Now follow the instructions.

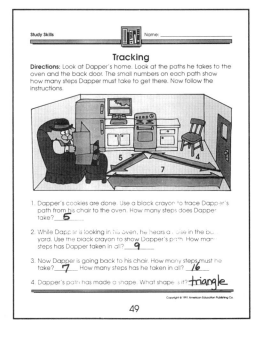

1. Dapper's cookies are done. Use a black crayon to trace Dapper's path from his chair to the oven. How many steps does Dapper take? **5**

2. While Dapper is looking in his oven, he hears a noise in the back yard. Use the black crayon to show Dapper's path. How many steps has Dapper taken in all? **9**

3. Now Dapper is going back to his chair. How many steps must he take? **7** How many steps has he taken in all? **16**

4. Dapper's path has made a shape. What shape is it? **triangle**

Review

Directions: Use the space below to draw a map of your neighborhood - - or any neighborhood. On your map, draw a school, a library, a home and a store. Then mark a path that tracks a path from (1) home to (2) school to (3) library to (4) store to (5) home.

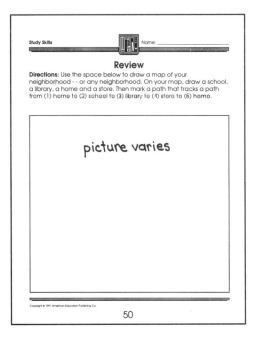

picture varies

Predicting Outcome

Directions: Read the story. Finish the last box. What will Jane do? What will she say?

1. "Do you want to go to the library with me?"
"Yes, I want a book about seashells."

2. "Good. Here is my book about space ships."

3. "Have you found your book?"
"No. I can't find it."
"Why don't you ask someone?"

4. What do you think Jane will do?

Answer varies

Predicting Outcome

Directions: Read the story. Use the last box to finish it.

1. "Look at that elephant! He sure is big!"

2. "I'm hungry."
"I bet that elephant is, too."

3. "Stop Tess! Look at that sign!"

4. What will Tom and Tess do?

Answer varies

81

Predicting Outcome

Directions: Read the story. Finish the story the way you think it should end. Then color your pcture.

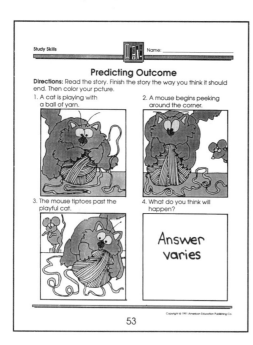

1. A cat is playing with a ball of yarn.
2. A mouse begins peeking around the corner.
3. The mouse tiptoes past the playful cat.
4. What do you think will happen?

Answer varies

53

Making Inferences

Directions: Read the story. Then answer the questions.

Tom is baking cookies. He wears special clothes when he bakes. He puts flour, sugar, eggs and butter into a bowl. He mixes everything together. He puts them in the oven at 11:15 a.m. It takes them 15 minutes to bake. Tom wants something cold and white to drink when he eats his cookies.

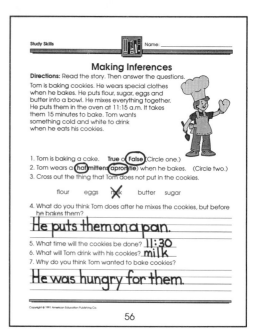

1. Tom is baking a cake. True or (False) (Circle one.)
2. Tom wears a (hat) mittens (apron) tie when he bakes. (Circle two.)
3. Cross out the thing that Tom does not put in the cookies.

    flour   eggs   ✗   butter   sugar

4. What do you think Tom does after he mixes the cookies, but before he bakes them?

He puts them on a pan.

5. What time will the cookies be done? **11:30**
6. What will Tom drink with his cookies? **milk**
7. Why do you think Tom wanted to bake cookies?

He was hungry for them.

56

Making Inferences

Directions: Read the story. Answer the questions.

Mrs. Posey is looking forward to a visit from Grandma Dapper. That morning, she cleans her house. She bakes a cherry pie. An hour before Grandma Dapper is to arrive, the phone rings. Mrs. Posey says she understands. But she looks very sad.

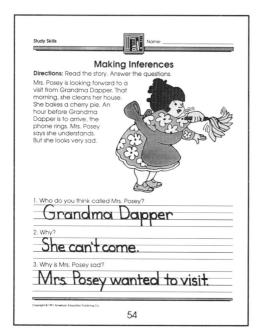

1. Who do you think called Mrs. Posey?

Grandma Dapper

2. Why?

She can't come.

3. Why is Mrs. Posey sad?

Mrs Posey wanted to visit.

54

Making Inferences

Directions: Read the story. Answer the questions.

Jane and her family are on a trip. It is very sunny. Jane loves to swim. She also likes the waves. But there is something else she likes even more. Jane builds drip castles. She makes drips by using very wet sand. She lets it drip out of her hand into a tall pile. She makes the drip piles as high as she can.

1. Where is Jane?   **The beach**
2. What does Jane wear on her trip?   **Bathing suit**
3. Is Jane (hot) or **cold?** (circle one)
4. What does Jane like to do best?   **Build sand castles**
5. What are drip castle made from?   **Sand**
6. What do you think happens when drip castles get too big?   **They fall.**
7. If Jane gets too hot, what do you think she does?   **Goes swimming.**

57

Making Inferences

Directions: Read the story. Follow the instructions.

John and his Dad are going to a baseball game today. The game starts at 2:00 p.m. John wakes up at 9:00 a.m. He has a swimming class at 10:30. His class is over at 11:30 a.m. John has lunch at noon. Then he must clean his room. Dad says, "We must leave at 1:30." But John wants to play with his friend, too. Dad says, "Play after you clean your room, but before we leave for the game."

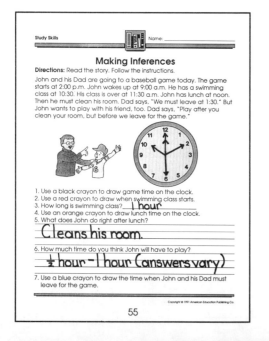

1. Use a black crayon to draw game time on the clock.
2. Use a red crayon to draw when swimming class starts.
3. How long is swimming class? **1 hour**
4. Use an orange crayon to draw lunch time on the clock.
5. What does John do right after lunch?

Cleans his room.

6. How much time do you think John will have to play?

½ hour - 1 hour (answers vary)

7. Use a blue crayon to draw the time when John and his Dad must leave for the game.

55

Review

Directions: Look at each question. Follow the instructions.

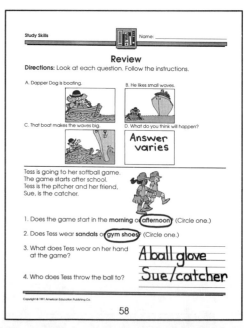

A. Dapper Dog is boating.
B. He likes small waves.
C. That boat makes the waves big.
D. What do you think will happen?

Answer varies

Tess is going to her softball game. The game starts after school. Tess is the pitcher and her friend, Sue, is the catcher.

1. Does the game start in the **morning** or (afternoon) (Circle one.)
2. Does Tess wear **sandals** or (gym shoes) (Circle one.)
3. What does Tess wear on her hand at the game?   **A ball glove**
4. Who does Tess throw the ball to?   **Sue/catcher**

58

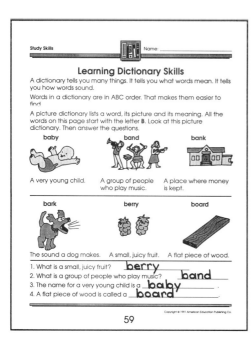

Learning Dictionary Skills

A dictionary tells you many things. It tells you what words mean. It tells you how words sound.

Words in a dictionary are in ABC order. That makes them easier to find.

A picture dictionary lists a word, its picture and its meaning. All the words on this page start with the letter **B**. Look at this picture dictionary. Then answer the questions.

baby — A very young child.

band — A group of people who play music.

bank — A place where money is kept.

bark — The sound a dog makes.

berry — A small, juicy fruit.

board — A flat piece of wood.

1. What is a small, juicy fruit? **berry**
2. What is a group of people who play music? **band**
3. The name for a very young child is a **baby**
4. A flat piece of wood is called a **board**

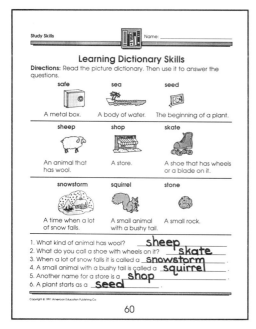

Learning Dictionary Skills

Directions: Read the picture dictionary. Then use it to answer the questions.

safe — A metal box.

sea — A body of water.

seed — The beginning of a plant.

sheep — An animal that has wool.

shop — A store.

skate — A shoe that has wheels or a blade on it.

snowstorm — A time when a lot of snow falls.

squirrel — A small animal with a bushy tail.

stone — A small rock.

1. What kind of animal has wool? **sheep**
2. What do you call a shoe with wheels on it? **skate**
3. When a lot of snow falls it is called a **snowstorm**
4. A small animal with a bushy tail is called a **squirrel**
5. Another name for a store is a **shop**
6. A plant starts as a **seed**

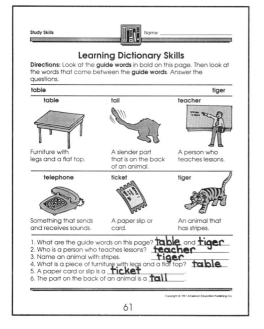

Learning Dictionary Skills

Directions: Look at the **guide words** in bold on this page. Then look at the words that come between the **guide words**. Answer the questions.

table   **tiger**

table — Furniture with legs and a flat top.

tail — A slender part that is on the back of an animal.

teacher — A person who teaches lessons.

telephone — Something that sends and receives sounds.

ticket — A paper slip or card.

tiger — An animal that has stripes.

1. What are the guide words on this page? **table** and **tiger**
2. Who is a person who teaches lessons? **teacher**
3. Name an animal with stripes. **tiger**
4. What is a piece of furniture with legs and a flat top? **table**
5. A paper card or slip is a **ticket**
6. The part on the back of an animal is a **tail**

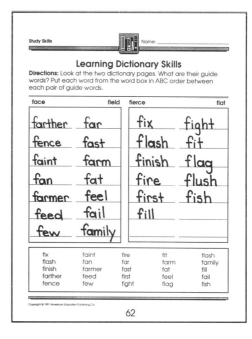

Learning Dictionary Skills

Directions: Look at the two dictionary pages. What are their guide words? Put each word from the word box in ABC order between each pair of guide words.

face	field	fierce	flat
farther	far	fix	fight
fence	fast	flash	fit
faint	farm	finish	flag
fan	fat	fire	flush
farmer	feel	first	fish
feed	fail	fill	
few	family		

fix	faint	fire	fit	flash
flash	fan	far	farm	family
finish	farmer	fast	fat	fill
farther	feed	first	feel	fail
fence	few	fight	flag	fish

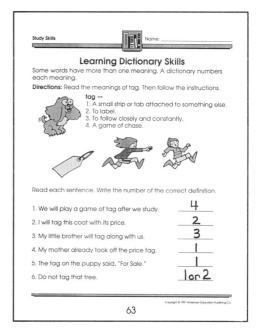

Learning Dictionary Skills

Some words have more than one meaning. A dictionary numbers each meaning.

Directions: Read the meanings of tag. Then follow the instructions.

tag —
1. A small strip or tab attached to something else.
2. To label.
3. To follow closely and constantly.
4. A game of chase.

Read each sentence. Write the number of the correct definition.

1. We will play a game of tag after we study. **4**
2. I will tag this coat with its price. **2**
3. My little brother will tag along with us. **3**
4. My mother already took off the price tag. **1**
5. The tag on the puppy said, "For Sale." **1**
6. Do not tag that tree. **1 or 2**

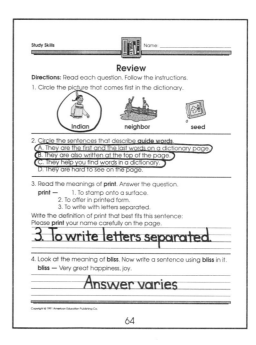

Review

Directions: Read each question. Follow the instructions.

1. Circle the picture that comes first in the dictionary.

Indian (circled)   **neighbor**   **seed**

2. Circle the sentences that describe **guide words**.
   - A. They are the first and the last words on a dictionary page. (circled)
   - B. They are also written at the top of the page. (circled)
   - C. They help you find words in a dictionary. (circled)
   - D. They are hard to see on the page.

3. Read the meanings of **print**. Answer the question.

print —
1. To stamp onto a surface.
2. To offer in printed form.
3. To write with letters separated.

Write the definition of print that best fits this sentence:
Please **print** your name carefully on the page.

3. To write letters separated.

4. Look at the meaning of **bliss**. Now write a sentence using **bliss** in it.

bliss — Very great happiness, joy.

Answer varies

INTRODUCING
BRIGHTER CHILD™ SOFTWARE!

BRIGHTER CHILD ™ SOFTWARE for Windows

These colorful and exciting programs teach basic skills in an entertaining way. They are based on the best selling BRIGHTER CHILD™ workbooks, written and designed by experts who are also parents. Sound is included to facilitate learning, but it is not nesessary to run these programs. BRIGHTER CHILD™ software has received many outstanding reviews and awards. All Color! Easy to use!

The following programs are each sold separately in a 3.5 disk format.

Reading & Phonics Grade 1	*Reading Grade 2*	*Reading Grade 3*
Math Grade 1	*Math Grade 2*	*Math Grade 3*

CD-ROM Titles!

These new titles combine three grade levels of a subject on one CD-ROM! Each CD contains more than 80 different activities packed with colors and sound.

Reading and Phonics Challenge - CD-ROM Grades 1, 2, 3

Math Challenge - CD-ROM Grades 1, 2, 3

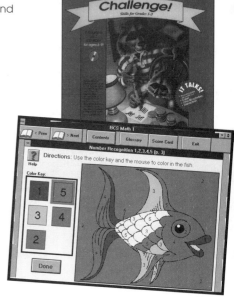

JIM HENSON'S MUPPET™/
BRIGHTER CHILD™ SOFTWARE for Windows™

Based on the best selling Muppet Press™/BRIGHTER CHILD™ Workbooks, these software programs for Windows are designed to teach basic concepts to children in preschool and kindergarten. Children will develop phonics skills and critical and creative thinking skills, and more! No reading is required with a sound card -- the directions are read aloud. The Muppet™ characters are universally known and loved and are recognized as having high educational value.

The following programs are each sold separately in a 3.5 disk format.
Each package contains:

- a program disk with more than 15 full color animated interactive lessons!
- sound is included which facilitates learning.
- Full-color workbook

Beginning Sounds: Phonics	*Letters: Capital & Small*
Same & Different	

CD-ROM Titles

Beginning Reading & Phonics- CD-ROM

This title combines three different MUPPET™/BRIGHTER CHILD™ Software programs -- Beginning Sounds: Phonics, Letters, and Same and Different -- all on one CD-ROM! This valuable software contains more than 50 different activities packed with color, sound, and interactive animation!

Reading & Phonics II- CD-ROM

Three Muppet™ Early Reading Programs on one CD-ROM. Includes *Sorting & Ordering*, *Thinking Skills*, and *Sound Patterns: More Phonics*

Available at stores everywhere.

OVERVIEW

ENRICHMENT READING is designed to provide children with practice in reading and to increase students' reading abilities. The program consists of six editions, one each for grades 1 through 6. The major areas of reading instruction—word skills, vocabulary, study skills, comprehension, and literary forms—are covered as appropriate at each level.

ENRICHMENT READING provides a wide range of activities that target a variety of skills in each instructional area. The program is unique because it helps children expand their skills in playful ways with games, puzzles, riddles, contests, and stories. The high-interest activities are informative and fun to do.

Home involvement is important to any child's success in school. *ENRICHMENT READING* is the ideal vehicle for fostering home involvement. Every lesson provides specific opportunities for children to work with a parent, a family member, an adult, or a friend.

AUTHORS

Peggy Kaye, the author of *ENRICHMENT READING*, is also an author of *ENRICHMENT MATH* and the author of two parent/teacher resource books, *Games for Reading* and *Games for Math*. Currently, Ms. Kaye divides her time between writing books and tutoring students in reading and math. She has also taught for ten years in New York City public and private schools.

WRITERS

Timothy J. Baehr is a writer and editor of instructional materials on the elementary, secondary, and college levels. Mr. Baehr has also authored an award-winning column on bicycling and a resource book for writers of educational materials.

Cynthia Benjamin is a writer of reading instructional materials, television scripts, and original stories. Ms. Benjamin has also tutored students in reading at the New York University Reading Institute.

Russell Ginns is a writer and editor of materials for a children's science and nature magazine. Mr. Ginn's speciality is interactive materials, including games, puzzles, and quizzes.

WHY ENRICHMENT READING?

Enrichment and parental involvement are both crucial to children's success in school, and educators recognize the important role work done at home plays in the educational process. Enrichment activities give children opportunities to practice, apply, and expand their reading skills, while encouraging them to think while they read. *ENRICHMENT READING* offers exactly this kind of opportunity. Each lesson focuses on an important reading skill and involves children in active learning. Each lesson will entertain and delight children.

When childen enjoy their lessons and are involved in the activities, they are naturally alert and receptive to learning. They understand more. They remember more. All children enjoy playing games, having contests, and solving puzzles. They like reading interesting stories, amusing stories, jokes, and riddles. Activities such as these get children involved in reading. This is why these kinds of activities form the core of *ENRICHMENT READING*.

Each lesson consists of two parts. Children complete the first part by themselves. The second part is completed together with a family member, an adult, or a friend. *ENRICHMENT READING* activities do not require people at home to teach reading. Instead, the activities involve everyone in enjoyable reading games and interesting language experiences.

ENRICHMENT ANSWER KEY
Reading Grade 2

Page 65   *Red:* big/large, sad/unhappy, world/earth, road/street, thin/skinny, yell/shout *Blue:* gate/coat, door/rug, cat/dog, car/swing, fork/water, food/bed, spin/log

Page 66   *Items with* ✔: 1. 2. 6. 7. 9. *Possible answers:* 3. well 4. far 5. low 8. cloudy, shady, snowy 10. early 11. old

Page 67   Turn on the *fan.* Open a *can* of beans. I need my baseball *bat.* I *can* buy that robot. The car must turn *left.* I need a *yard* of rope. How many apples are *left* on the plate? I worked hard and need to *rest.* Where are the *rest* of my toys? I am a rock-and-roll *fan.* A *bat* lives in a cave; yard; yes

Page 68   Answers will vary.

ENRICHMENT ANSWER KEY
Reading Grade 2

Page 69 *First suitcase:* Paul *Second suitcase:* Ana *Third suitcase:* Jill; answers will vary

Page 70 Answers will vary, but should indicate what might happen next in the story.

Page 71 Answers will vary.

Page 72 Return of the Cowhands, David Ash, OK Horse Ranch, no, 3:00 PM